Hello out there!

THE WRITTEN WORD

Janet Weller

Illustrated by Colin Mier

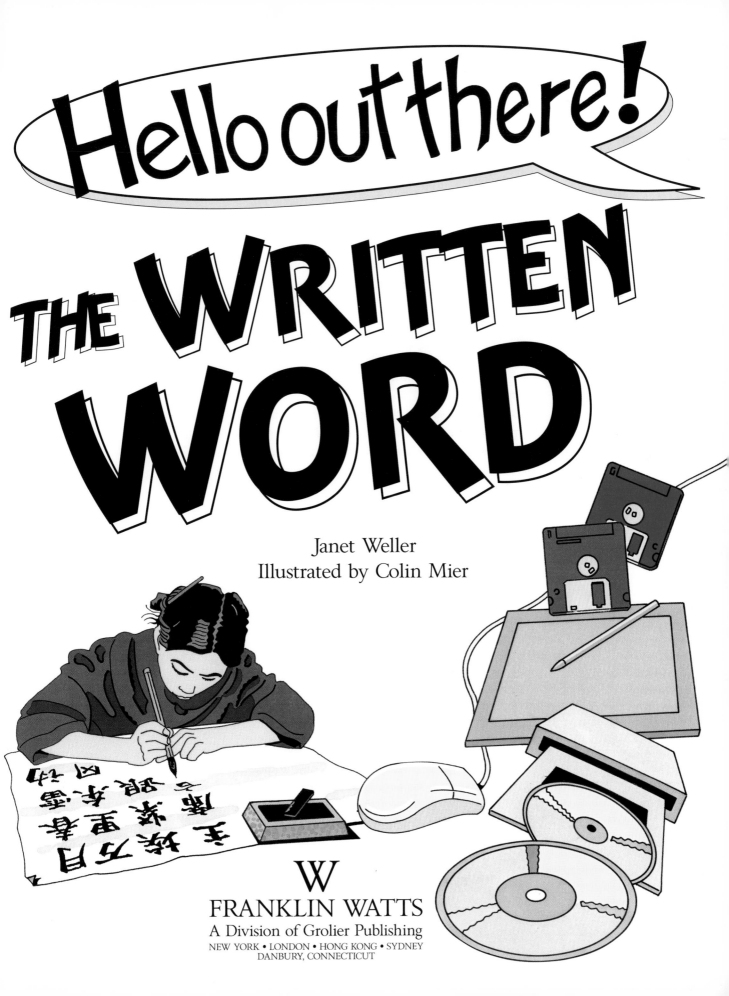

W

FRANKLIN WATTS

A Division of Grolier Publishing

NEW YORK • LONDON • HONG KONG • SYDNEY
DANBURY, CONNECTICUT

© Franklin Watts 1997
First American Edition 1998 by
Franklin Watts, A Division of Grolier Publishing
90 Sherman Turnpike, Danbury, CT 06816
Visit Franklin Watts on the Internet at:
http://publishing.grolier.com

Weller, Janet.
    The written word / Janet Weller.
        p.   cm. -- (Hello out there!)
Includes index.
    Summary: Discusses the importance of writing as a method of
communication with emphasis on its different forms, the development
of the alphabet, calligraphy, writing implements, graphology, and
the invention of printing.
    ISBN 0-531-14470-4
    1. Written communication--Juvenile literature. 2. Writing-
-Juvenile literature. 3. Psychology, Comparative--Juvenile
literature. [1. Writing.] I. Title. II. Series.
P211.W35 1997
302.2'244--DC21   97-280
                                                             CIP
                                                              AC

Series editor: Rachel Cooke
Designer: Melissa Alaverdy
Picture research: Sarah Snashall

Printed in Belgium
Picture acknowledgments:
Ancient Art and Architecture/Ronald Sheridan
cover background, pp. 8, 10bl, 14, 15, 22, 23 both;
AKG Photo pp. 6, 21 both;
Bridgeman Art Library p. 10 cr (Giraudon);
e.t. archive pp. 7 (Archaeological Museum Lima),
13 (Histoisk Museet Stockholm);
The Image Bank p. 25 (Bernard Roussel); Ray Moller p. 26;
Steve Shott cover bl & br, pp. 5, 19;
Telegraph Colour Library pp. 17, 27.

Contents

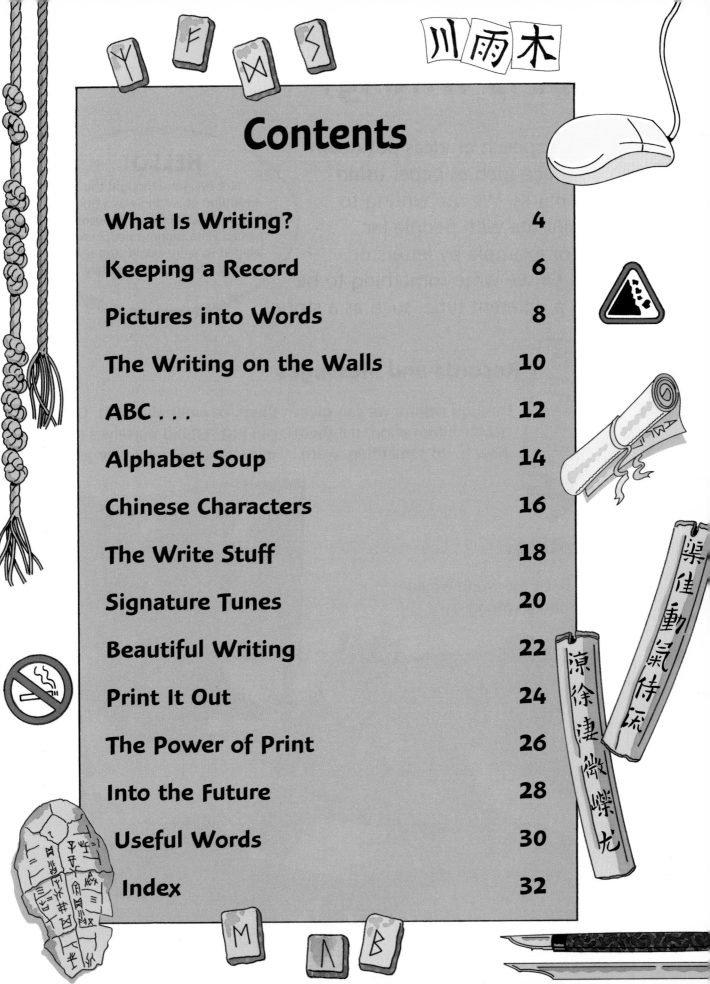

What Is Writing?

Writing is speech or ideas put down on a surface such as paper using special marks. We use writing to communicate with people far away, for example by letters or **e-mail**. Or we write something to be read at a different time, such as a story.

HELLO!

Not everyone thought the invention of writing was a good thing. An Ancient Greek **philosopher** named Plato thought people who learned to write would stop using their memories completely.

Records and Messages

Through writing we can give people information, tell them how to do something, warn them, or entertain them. Or we can just remind ourselves of something we might forget.

No Writing?

Imagine what the world would be like without writing:

When Did Writing Begin?

Writing began to appear in several different parts of the world between 3,000 and 5,000 years ago. The first writing was used to keep records of goods, food, supplies, and animals.

Different peoples have invented different ways of writing their languages. These newspapers show a few examples.

Learning to Write

Learning to write—and to read—takes time.

aA bB cC dD eE FF gG hH iI jJ kK lLmM oO pPqQrR sS tT uU vV wW xX yY zZ

Children must learn the different signs or letters and how these match the spoken sounds they already know.

Then they must learn ▶ to spell: how to put the signs or letters together to make words.

C-a-t spells CAT.

And they must learn ▶ **grammar**: how to put the words into sentences which will mean something to another reader.

My Cat sleeps all day.

Why Is Writing Important?

Before television and radio, writing was the best way of passing information from one group of people to another at a distance and over time. If scientists and inventors had not written about their work and others had not read about it, television and radio would probably never have been invented!

5

Keeping a Record

Thousands of years ago, prehistoric artists decorated caves with pictures of animals they hunted. Sometimes they put other marks and lines next to these pictures. These marks were the beginning of writing.

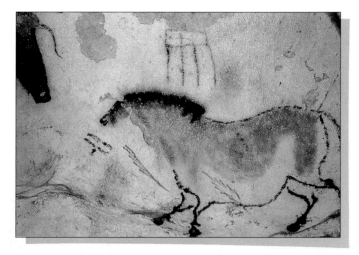

▲ These cave paintings from Lascaux in France date from about 15,000 BC.

Trade and Taxes

About 10,000 years ago, people began to live in towns and cities. They traded with each other and paid **taxes** to their rulers who protected them. Traders and farmers wanted to remember what they had bought and sold and the taxes they had paid. Writing was needed to keep a record of trade and administration.

HELLO!
History begins with writing—we call the time before people began keeping written records prehistory!

◄ Some prehistoric people scratched tallies on eagle bones. These tallies probably recorded how the moon changed shape in a month.

Tallies

Tallies are an early kind of very simple writing. People could keep a record using a line or mark to stand for a number. The more lines or marks, the bigger the number.

◄ You probably still use tallies in math and science lessons at school.

▲ The **British Treasury** used tally sticks to record payments from 1100 until 1834. The different-sized notches stood for different amounts of money.

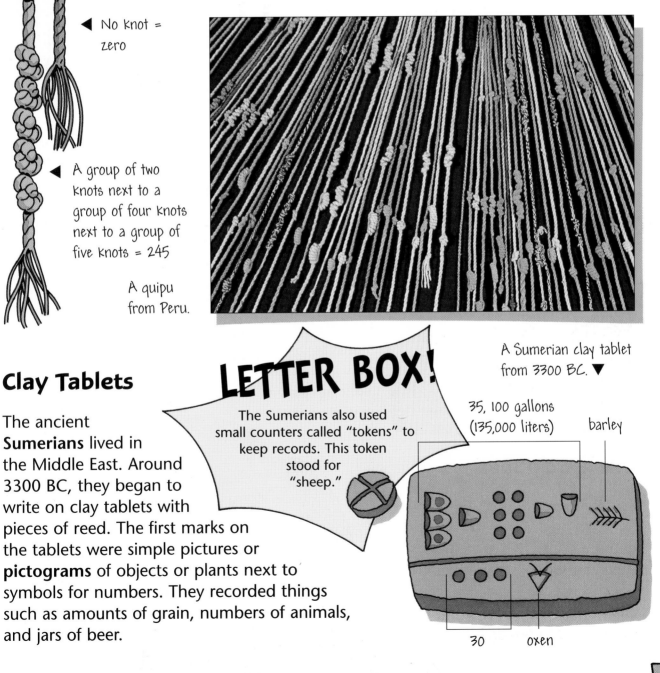

HELLO!

The Incas never invented a writing system for their language. Inca children who went to school had to recite after the teacher and learn everything by heart!

Quipus

The Inca people of Peru kept track of money and materials using a set of knotted strings called a quipu (pronounced kweepoo). Different colors of string stood for different things, for example, a yellow string stood for gold and a white string for silver. Different groups of knots stood for different numbers.

◀ No knot = zero

◀ A group of two knots next to a group of four knots next to a group of five knots = 245

A quipu from Peru.

Clay Tablets

The ancient **Sumerians** lived in the Middle East. Around 3300 BC, they began to write on clay tablets with pieces of reed. The first marks on the tablets were simple pictures or **pictograms** of objects or plants next to symbols for numbers. They recorded things such as amounts of grain, numbers of animals, and jars of beer.

LETTER BOX!

The Sumerians also used small counters called "tokens" to keep records. This token stood for "sheep."

A Sumerian clay tablet from 3300 BC. ▼

35, 100 gallons (135,000 liters)   barley

30   oxen

Pictures into Words

Using pictures for messages can be very useful. We still use pictograms to get information quickly. Some pictograms can be understood by anyone, no matter what language they speak.

Universal Pictures

What do these signs mean and where would you see them?

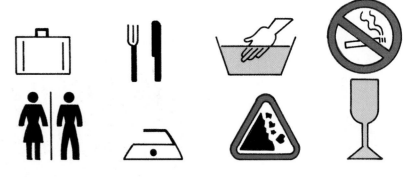

Changing Shapes

From 3000–600 BC, the pictograms on Sumerian clay tablets slowly changed into **abstract** signs, which no longer looked like real things.

3000 BC	2100 BC	1800 BC	600 BC

= OX

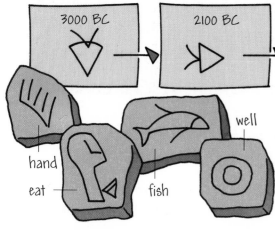

hand

eat

fish

well

◀ This change was partly because early pictograms could be confusing, like some of these examples. It was also because it was slow and difficult to draw realistic pictures on wet clay.

Wedge Shapes

For their new style of writing the Sumerians used a reed with the end cut in a slant. This gave Sumerian writing a wedge-shaped look. For this reason it is called *cuneiform*, from *cuneus*, the Latin word for wedge.

Writing Ideas

The Sumerians found it difficult to write about things they couldn't draw pictures of, such as feelings and ideas, or times like "tomorrow." They solved this problem by using rebuses. A **rebus** is a picture for a word that has one sound but more than one meaning.

The Sumerian word for arrow also meant life. So to write "life," the Sumerian scribes used the pictogram or cuneiform sign for "arrow." The Sumerians also used rebuses for the separate **syllables** of longer words.

HELLO!
The word *rebus* comes from a Latin phrase *non verbis sed rebus* which means *not by words but by things.*

These two cuneiform signs both stand for one everyday thing and one abstract thing.

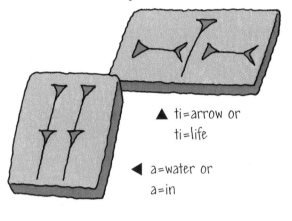

▲ ti=arrow or ti=life

◄ a=water or a=in

Activity

Make some simple picture signs for different places in your school or home, for example, the cafeteria, the bathroom, or your bedroom.

Using Rebuses

Write some rebus messages for your friends. Here are some ideas:

◄ A picture of an eye could stand for the word "I."

◄ A picture of a deer could stand for the word "dear."

Try making long words with picture syllables:

Put a bee and a leaf together to make the word "belief."

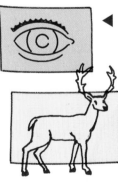

The Writing on the Walls

Ancient Egyptian writing began soon after the first Sumerian writing. It consisted of small symbols and pictures which we now call **hieroglyphs**. Hieroglyphs were used by the Egyptians for 3,000 years.

Tomb Decorations

The Ancient Egyptians were very religious and they had strong beliefs about life after death. They built many large temples and tombs, which they decorated with sacred writings in hieroglyphs, such as Queen Nefertari's tomb (right). But by the 6th century AD, everyone had forgotten what hieroglyphs meant.

A Mystery Solved

In 1823, a Frenchman named Jean-François Champollion solved the mystery of Egyptian hieroglyphs. In 1799 French soldiers had found an interesting stone set into an old wall in Egypt. This was the Rosetta Stone.

The Rosetta Stone had the same piece of writing carved on it in ancient Greek and in Egyptian hieroglyphs. Champollion knew Greek so he could decode the hieroglyphs.

Activity

Use the "sound" hieroglyphs opposite to write your name. Match the sounds rather than the spelling.

Here is an example:

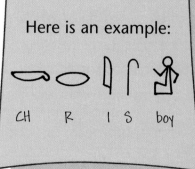

CH   R   I   S   boy

Champollion discovered that hieroglyphic
signs were used in different ways.

Some signs were pictograms:

= walk, go   = bee

Some signs were
used as rebuses:

was pronounced "wer" and meant
swallow, but it also meant **great**.

Some signs gave extra clues about tricky words that
had more than one meaning. For example:

was pronounced "wen" and
meant **open** and **hurry**.

To make the right meaning of "wen" clear, other
signs were added to it:

With the sign for **door**, the
meaning of "wen" was **open**.

With the sign for **go**, the
meaning of "wen" was **hurry**.

And some signs were used just for their sound.
The hieroglyphs around the page made sounds
similar to the letters we use:

i

j

k

l

m

n

o

p

q

r

h

g

f/v

e

d

b

a

z

y/"ee"

u/w

t

s

For "c" use
the signs for
"k" or "s."
For "x" use
the signs for
"k + s."

= boy   = girl   ch   sh

ABC . . .

Alphabets are a series of signs for single sounds rather than signs for words or syllables like those the Sumerians and ancient Egyptians used. With alphabets, you can learn how to write about 20–35 letters (26 in English) and to combine them in different ways to make words.

Initial Letters

A kind of alphabet first appeared in the ancient Middle East in about 1600 BC, but nobody is very sure who invented it. The story of the modern alphabet begins with the **Phoenicians**, who traded and traveled all over the Mediterranean and beyond. They took their alphabet with them wherever they went.

1000 BC

The Phoenicians were the first people to use the letters which became our alphabet.

700 BC

The Ancient Greeks adapted the Phoenician idea to write their language.

The alphabet's journey

Black Sea

Ancient Greeks

Italy

Etruscans

Greece

Romans

Phoenicians

Mediterranean Sea

500 BC

The **Etruscans** took the Greek alphabet, changed it a bit more . . .

400 BC

. . . and passed it to the Romans.

They passed the "Roman" alphabet to us!

Reading the Runes

Like the Phoenicians, the Vikings were great travelers and traders. They probably saw the Roman alphabet on their travels and invented the **runic alphabet** to write inscriptions on monuments,

A Viking's axe, helmet and brooch could be decorated with runes.

weapons, and jewelry.

The Vikings took the runic alphabet to Britain when they invaded in the 9th century. As a result Old English was once written in runic letters.

The Runic Alphabet

A	B	D	E	F	G	H	I	J	K	L

M	N	O	P	R	S	T	TH	U	W	Z

Activity

Read this Runic message and find out what the Runic alphabet is called:

Write your own message using the runic alphabet.

The runes around this Viking memorial stone from Sweden dedicate it to Rodvisl.

Alphabet Soup

Alphabets are a very adaptable system of writing; they can be used to write down all sorts of different-sounding languages. Today most countries in the world, except China and Japan, use some sort of alphabet for their writing.

Many alphabets look rather different from the Roman alphabet used for English.

◀ Arabic

أطيب التحيات من مصر

Italian ▶

Ciao dall' Italia

Hebrew
▼

שלום

מישראל

Russian
▼

Привет из России

ભારતથી

નમસ્કાર

▲
Gujarati

Saintly Script

Russian is written in the Cyrillic alphabet. It is named after a Greek missionary called Saint Cyril, who invented a **script** for writing **Slavonic languages** in the 9th century. It let Slavic people read the Bible and other Christian texts, like the one in this sacred painting, in their own language. Based on the Greek alphabet, Cyril's script has developed into the modern Russian alphabet.

LETTER BOX!

The alphabet with the most letters belongs to the Khmer language, which is spoken in Kampuchea (Cambodia). It has 74 letters, although some of these have no current use!

Leaving Out Vowels

The Arabic alphabet developed from the same Phoenician alphabet as the Roman alphabet. Arabic is written from right to left and does not usually show the **vowels**. Small signs for vowels may be written above and below each word but Arab children eventually have to learn to leave them out.

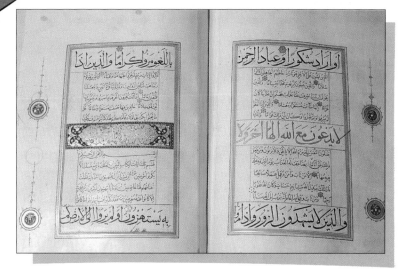

The Koran, the **Muslim** holy book, is written in Arabic.

Why Is Spelling Hard?

Although alphabets are a very practical way of writing, they are not always perfect. For example, English spelling is sometimes difficult because some sounds are written down in many different ways and some letters are pronounced in several different ways.

This is because spoken and written English have changed a lot over hundreds of years. But some things are spelled exactly as we hear them. For example: get, sit, Sam. A word that is spelled the way it sounds is spelled **phonetically**.

LETTER BOX!

Rotokas, which is spoken on Bougainville Island in Papua New Guinea, has only 11 letters in its alphabet: a, b, e, g, i, k, o, p, r, t, and u.

Inventing Alphabets

In 1444 King Sejong of Korea invented a new alphabet for the Korean language. Before this, Korean was written in Chinese characters.

The new alphabet was called "Hangul" and had 28 letters. The king told his subjects that he personally had created it so that they would be too scared not to use it!

Chinese Characters

Chinese writing began around 1200 BC and has stayed almost the same for 3,000 years. This makes it the oldest writing system still used in the world.

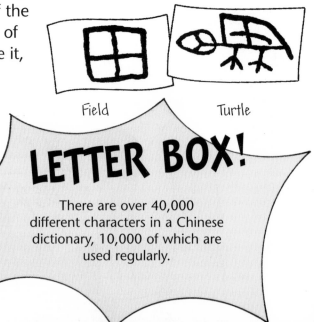

Chinese was sometimes written on bamboo. This may explain why Chinese is written vertically instead of horizontally.

Fortune Tellers

Chinese was first written on ox-bones used to tell fortunes. The ox-bones were heated until they cracked. Then the fortune-tellers would "read" the cracks and say what was going to happen in the future. They then wrote the "fortune" on the bone.

▲ Some fortunes were written on turtle shells like this one.

Full of Character

Chinese writing doesn't use an alphabet. Each sign or "**character**" corresponds to a word. Part of the character gives you a clue about the meaning of the word and part tells you how to pronounce it, a bit like some Egyptian hieroglyphs.

Some early Chinese characters were pictograms. Like Sumerian pictograms these soon became more abstract.

Field   Turtle

Examples of Chinese characters and their meanings:

River   Rain   Tree

LETTER BOX!

There are over 40,000 different characters in a Chinese dictionary, 10,000 of which are used regularly.

A Feat of Memory

Because there are so many characters, it takes a long time to learn to write Chinese. For this reason, the Chinese government introduced "Pinyin" ("spell sound") in 1958. Pinyin is a set of about 30 letters which match the sounds of Chinese. Pinyin is now used alongside Chinese characters, for example for typing Chinese into computers.

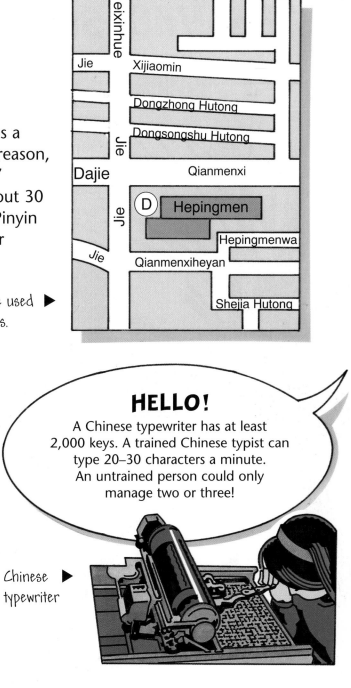

Pinyin words are used ▶ on Chinese maps.

HELLO!
A Chinese typewriter has at least 2,000 keys. A trained Chinese typist can type 20–30 characters a minute. An untrained person could only manage two or three!

Chinese ▶ typewriter

In Japan you often see Chinese characters, syllable signs and Roman letters all together.

Complex Japanese

Japanese has more than one kind of writing system. It uses about 2,000 Chinese characters, plus two different sets of 46 signs which stand for syllables like "ka", "sa", "ta," and "na." This probably makes Japanese writing the hardest of all to learn.

The Write Stuff

In order to write you need something to write with and a surface to write on. Characters and letters have been written with many different tools and on many different surfaces.

Papyrus

For almost 4,000 years **papyrus** was the main writing material used in the Middle East and around the Mediterranean. The Egyptians first made papyrus from the stem of the papyrus plant which grew along the banks of the Nile River.

◀ Papyrus plant

1 Papyrus was made by cutting a papyrus stem into thin strips.

2 Two layers of strips were then pressed together until they stuck.

The Egyptians wrote with brushes but the ancient Greeks invented ◀ reed pens.

Animal Skins

When papyrus became scarce, people used prepared animal skins. Parchment was made from sheepskin which was washed, scraped, stretched, and dried.

Parchment had a very smooth ▶ writing surface. It was used in Europe until the late Middle Ages.

Scribes wrote on parchment with quill pens made from goose feathers. ▶

Paper

Around AD 105 a Chinese official called Cai Lun invented a new writing material made from old rags—paper.

Paper is still made in roughly the same way today as it was by Cai Lun, except that now machines are used.

Making Paper

A pulp made from wetted wood or vegetable fibers is spread over a screen.

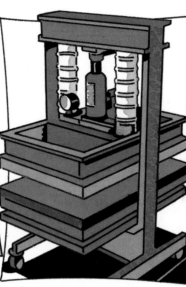

The pulp is then pressed to squeeze out the water.

The resulting sheet is then dried to make a piece of paper.

HELLO!
The very first sheets of Chinese paper were made from a pulp of mulberry bark, fishnets, and old sandals!

Pen Power

The problem with quill pens and later metal pens was that you had to dip them in ink every few seconds. In the 19th century fountain pens were invented. These had a container for ink inside them—no more dipping!

HELLO!
In 1938 George and Lazlo Biró invented a pen which could be thrown away when the ink inside was all used up. It was soon known as a biro.

The nib of a modern fountain pen is very similar to the point of the reed pen invented by the ancient Greeks.

Signature Tunes

Although we all learn to form the letters or characters of our language in the same way, the style of everyone's handwriting changes over time until it becomes unique to them.

Unique Writing

Handwriting experts called **graphologists** look closely at a person's handwriting to see what makes it different from someone else's.

Graphologists sometimes use this knowledge to help the police track down criminals such as forgers or blackmailers.

Other graphologists believe they can describe someone's personality just by looking at their handwriting.

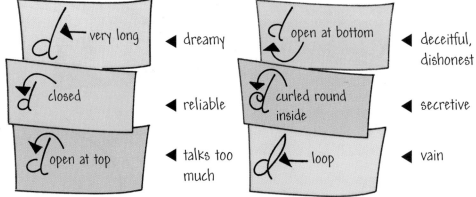

very long ◄ dreamy

closed ◄ reliable

open at top ◄ talks too much

open at bottom ◄ deceitful, dishonest

curled round inside ◄ secretive

loop ◄ vain

He thinks big and he likes attention!

What is Zak Like

Fooling the Experts

In the 1980s, the diaries of Adolf Hitler were discovered. Hitler was the dictator of Germany during World War II and had died in 1945. Were the diaries really his?

Expert graphologists said the diaries were genuine, but scientific tests proved them wrong. They showed that the paper and ink used for the diaries were modern—the paper had been stained with tea to make it look old. All the diaries had been forged!

Signed and Sealed

Everyone has a personal signature which they can use to sign letters and documents.

A signature is unique and shows that a person has read and agreed to a piece of writing, or it proves they are who they say they are—like on a credit card!

Fancy Flourishes

In the past, people often had very fancy signatures. This was partly to prevent other people from forging them. Signatures were also an important way for composers, such as Johann Sebastian Bach (right), or artists to say a piece of music or a painting was by them. What reasons can you think of

Activity
Compare your handwriting with a friend's. What is similar and what is different? Does your handwriting tell you anything about your personality?

Beautiful Writing

Many languages, such as Chinese and Arabic, are famous for their beautiful writing or **calligraphy**. People have taken the abstract shapes of letters and characters and made them into a form of art.

Sacred Scripts

Muslim artists were not allowed to paint pictures of people and animals. Instead, they used calligraphy to decorate their mosques (right) or created animals from letters (above). The writings they used came from the Muslim holy book, the Koran.

LETTER BOX!

One Chinese calligrapher spent fifteen years learning to write just one character absolutely perfectly!

Calligraphy and flowers decorate a mosque in Iran.

Brushed Art

Chinese calligraphy is done with a brush and ink. Chinese people consider it one of the highest forms of Chinese art.

HELLO!

Despite its beauty, the Book of Kells is full of silly mistakes. The scribes usually didn't try to correct these mistakes. Instead they often drew funny men in the margins pointing out the mistakes to the reader!

Illuminated Letters

Many of the hand-written books of the Dark Ages and Middle Ages were decorated with intricate illustrations which we call **illuminations**. In particular, initial letters were illuminated with dazzling colors such as red, blue, and gold. One special blue was called ultramarine, which was made from a crushed semi-precious stone called lapis lazuli.

One of the most beautiful illuminated manuscripts is the Irish Book of Kells which was made around AD 700.

Activity

Design illuminated letters for your own initials.

Maya Writing

The Maya people lived in Central America from AD 250 to AD 900. At first sight their writing looks simply like lots of beautiful little pictures of animals and amazing patterns, such as in the example shown here. But we now know that these pictures and shapes have meanings and sounds, which match the language the Maya people spoke.

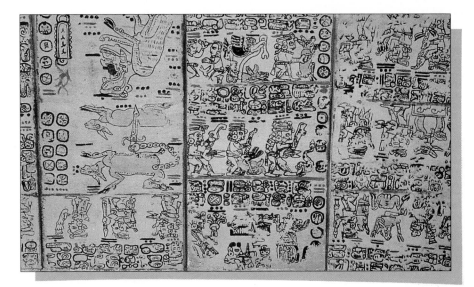

Print It Out

Making handwritten books was a very slow process. This meant that books were very expensive and only a few people could afford to buy them. Printing changed all that.

Sumerian seal

The Story of Printing

The Sumerians, the ancient Egyptians and the ancient Chinese all had seals. Seals could be pressed into wet clay, wax, or ink to make the same stamped mark over and over again.

By the 8th century AD, the Chinese had begun to use this idea for whole pages of writing and pictures.

1 First they carved the characters and pictures back to front into a big block of wood.

2 Then they covered this block with ink.

3 Then they pressed a piece of paper onto the block to make a printed page.

In the 11th century, a man called Pi-Sheng had the idea of using separate little clay blocks for each Chinese character. This was **movable type**.

In the 15th century, Johannes Gutenberg became the first person to use movable type in Europe. He used letters made from hot metal poured into molds.

When the metal had set hard, the letters were turned out. They could be put together to make words and sentences and used over and over again.

◄ Gutenberg's printing press

Hello out There!

Activity

Make "movable type" out of potato halves. Use them to print a poster.

Remember that letters which aren't symmetrical, like F, N, P, and so on, need to be cut the wrong way round. Otherwise when you print them they will be back to front!

Typecast

At first the letters in early printed books looked like handwritten ones. Later, special **typefaces** were invented for printing.

Jacoby Light • Jacoby Light Condensed • **Jacoby Black** • Jacoby Black Condensed
New Century Schoolbook • *Zaph Chancery* • Courier • Garamond Light
Garamond Light Italic • **Garamond Bold** • ***Garamond Bold Italic*** • Optima
Optima Oblique • **Optima Bold** • *Optima Bold Oblique* • Mead Regular
Mead Regular Italic • **Mead Bold** • ***Mead Bold Italic*** • **Helvetica Compressed**
Helvetica Roman • *Helvetica Roman Italic* • **Helvetica Bold**
Helvetica Bold Italic • Chicago • Gill Sans Regular • *Gill Sans Regular Italic*
Gill Sans Bold • *Gill Sans Bold Italic* • Times • Novarese Book
Novarese Book Italic • **Novarese Bold** • ***Novarese Bold Italic***
Lebensjoy Bold • Stone Serif Regular • *Stone Serif Regular Italic*
Stone Serif Bold • ***Stone Serif Bold Italic***

Now there are hundreds of different typefaces to choose from.

A Revolution in Print

Hand-operated printing presses like Gutenberg's remained in use for over 350 years. It was not until the 19th century that a new revolution in printing began.

Huge, steam-powered printing presses were invented that could print pages and pages of type on to huge rolls of paper. Printing became even quicker and cheaper.

Modern printing presses can handle several kilometres of paper at one time.

The Power of Print

Printing brought about great changes in people's lives. Words and the ideas they contained were now available to everyone, in cheaper books, newspapers, and advertisements.

HELLO!

The smallest book ever published was *Old King Cole!* in 1985. It was printed on paper measuring 1 mm by 1 mm. The pages can only be turned using a needle!

Easier Education

Cheaper books meant that more people—both children and grown-ups—could learn to read and write. Simple books teaching spelling, grammar, and religion were printed. Children's picture books, rhymes, and fairy-tales only began to appear about 250 years ago.

The Big Book of Children's Rhymes

Train

Apple

C is for CORN

D is for DUCK

In Full Color

Color printing began in the late 19th century. Color pictures are made up by printing layers of different colors—a bit like mixing paints. Special photographic machines **scan** an image to see which color should be printed where. These machines produce a piece of film of each color scanned: yellow, red, blue, and black.

◀ First a yellow layer is printed.

◀ Then a layer of red.

◀ Then a layer of blue.

◀ And finally a layer of black.

All the layers are then put together to produce a full color image.

New Ideas

Newspapers began to appear at the beginning of the 17th century. Suddenly, people could find out about what was happening in their own country and abroad. They could read about new ideas in religion and politics.

They often wanted to change things because of what they read.

LETTER BOX!

Nowadays companies can print a product name not just in newspaper and magazine advertisements, but on billboards, on posters, T-shirts, and mugs—in fact, just about anywhere.

Print All Around

The invention of printing also meant easier advertising. Manufacturers could put printed advertisements in newspapers and on walls and make sure that thousands of people knew all about their product.

Into the Future

In the modern world we are surrounded by information, not just from books, newspapers, and advertisements, but also from television, radio, and film. The printed word is not the only way of finding things out. And now a new kind of writing is grabbing even more of our attention.

Electronic Writing

Computers show us words on a screen instead of on a piece of paper. These words are not handwritten or printed but made up of lots of little bits of **electronic information**.

Millions of words can be stored invisibly in a computer's memory. Press a button and they appear on the screen.

Computers help us to record and sort out large amounts of written information very easily!

Return to menu.

The invention of the rocket has led to space travel. Find out more?

Launch spaceship.

CD ROMs are read on computers. They combine words with pictures and sound to give us a lot of information. You simply click on directions and instructions on screen to move around the disk.

Computer Printing

Today most books and newspapers are printed with the help of computers. Writers type their words onto a computer disk. A designer (like the one shown here) then moves the words around, adding pictures or photographs, to make the page of a book or a newspaper. This computer information can be used for printing.

Hello out there!

Hello out there

Already today there are computers which recognize words we speak and change them into writing on screen.

In the Crystal Ball

Some people predict that printed books will disappear completely, but others argue that books will still be used alongside computers. What do you think? Write down some predictions —you can look at them again in 50 years' time to see if they came true!

Where Next?

Writing on computers is very different from the writing on clay tablets the Sumerians made. How will we be writing thousands of years from now? And what will we be writing?

Here are a few predictions about writing in the future:

Paper newspapers will disappear. Instead they will be sent directly to our computer screens.

Instead of a book of printed instructions for our new washing machine we'll get a talking disk to put into our computer.

The **Internet** and **electronic voice mail** will replace letters sent through the mail.

Useful Words

alphabet: a writing system where letters stand for spoken sound.

abstract: not related to any object or action you can see or touch. Abstract words include words like good, tomorrow, and hope.

British Treasury: the part of the British government that looks after its money.

calligraphy: beautiful decorative hand-writing. It is written by a calligrapher.

CD ROM: Short for Compact Disk: Read Only Memory. A compact disk, used with a computer, stores information in written, visual, and sound form.

character: a sign in Chinese or Japanese writing.

e-mail: electronic mail. A typed message sent from one computer to another that are linked together on the worldwide computer network.

electronic information: information that is stored inside the memory of a computer as patterns of electronic pulses.

electronic voice mail: electronic mail that sends spoken messages.

Etruscans: the Etruscans lived in northern Italy from the 8th century BC until the 4th century BC.

grammar: the rules that control the way a language makes words and puts them together to make meaning.

graphologist: an expert on handwriting who can find the special characteristics of someone's writing. Some graphologists say they can describe someone's personality from their handwriting.

hieroglyph: a picture sign or symbol used in ancient Egyptian writing.

illumination: the art of decorating writing with colors, shapes, and pictures, widely practiced by Medieval scribes.

Internet: the international network of computers through which information can be gathered or written messages sent from one computer to another.

movable type: pieces of metal, each shaped like one letter of the alphabet or Chinese character, used for printing.

Muslim: someone whose religion is Islam and who is a follower of the prophet Muhammad.

papyrus: a plant that grows in Egypt and that can be used to make a kind of paper also called papyrus.

parchment: the skin of an animal (usually sheep) that has been specially prepared so that it can be used to write on.

philosopher: someone who thinks about the meaning of life and the proper way to live it.

Phoenicians: an ancient people who lived in the Middle East (around modern-day Lebanon) from 1250 BC to 500 BC.

phonetically: a word is written phonetically if its spelling matches exactly the way it is pronounced. For example: *sit* is spelled phonetically but *cough* is not.

pictogram: a sign in writing that is a picture of a real thing or action. Also, a modern sign that shows a simple picture standing for something, for example: a knife and fork standing for a restaurant.

rebus: a way of writing using pictures for words which have one sound but more than one meaning. For example, a picture of an eye can stand for both a real eye and the word *I*.

runic alphabet: the alphabet used by the Vikings and other peoples in northern Europe from the 3rd century to 10th century AD.

scan: machines such as computers scan something by moving a beam of light over a picture or word to get electronic information about it.

scribe: someone who writes for a living, copying documents or writing letters for others.

script: the marks used for a particular writing system, for example Roman letters or Chinese characters.

Slavonic languages: languages spoken by the Slavic peoples such as Russians, Poles, and Czechs.

Sumerians: an ancient people who lived in Mesopotamia (now in modern Iraq) from about 5000 BC until 2000 BC.

syllable: a part of a word that has a vowel sound and one or more consonants (the letters of an alphabet that are not vowels). For example, paper has two syllables—/pa/ and /per/.

taxes: money paid by people to rulers and governments. Taxes are used to pay for public services such as armies, roads, and drains.

typeface: a style of printed letters. For example, the typeface used here is called Stone. The typeface of the heading on the opposite page is called Lebensjoy.

vowels: the sounds of spoken words which we make without interrupting the flow of breath and the letters we use to represent these sounds in writing—in English, the letters *a*, *e*, *i*, *o*, and *u*.

Index